PEOPLE OF ALASKA

NORTH TO ALASKA

Lynn M. Stone

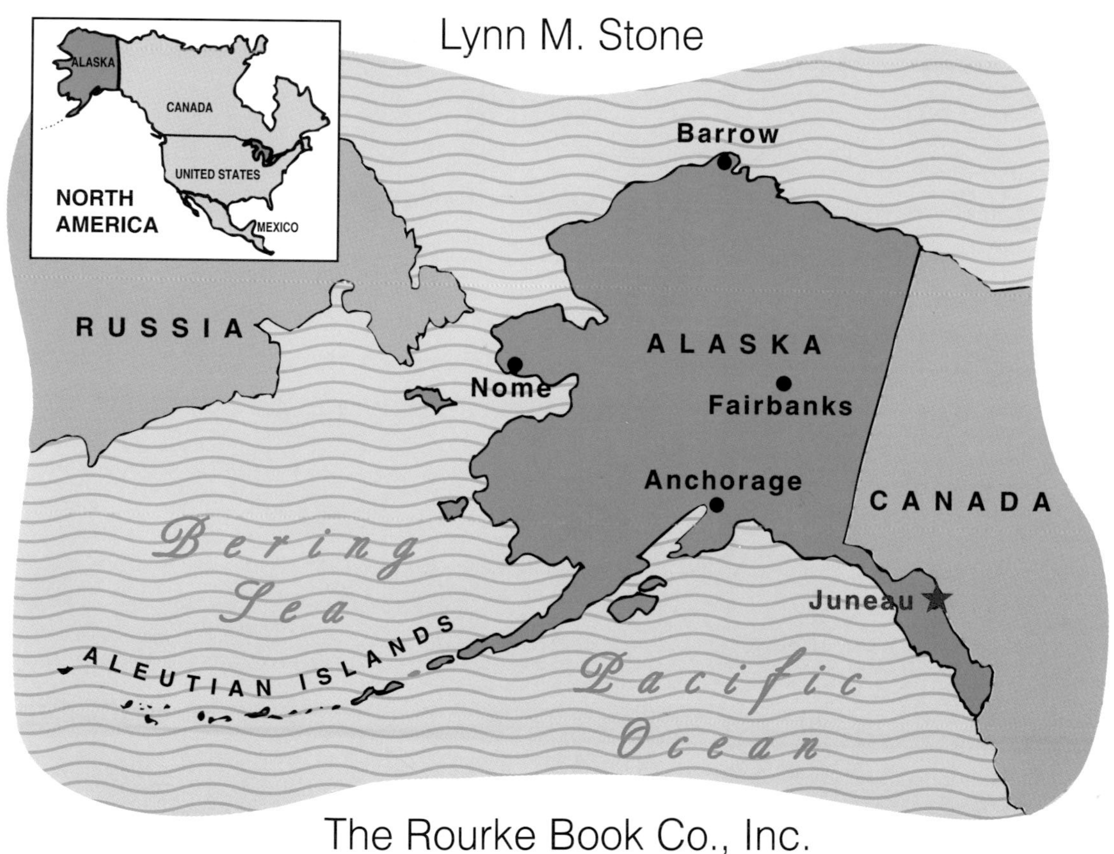

The Rourke Book Co., Inc.
Vero Beach, Florida 32964

Edited by Sandra A. Robinson

PHOTO CREDITS
Courtesy of Alaska Division of Tourism: cover, title page, pages 4, 7, 10, 12, 13 (Rex Melton), 15, 21; © Lynn M. Stone: pages 8, 17, 18

Library of Congress Cataloging-in-Publication Data

Stone, Lynn M.
People of Alaska / by Lynn M. Stone.
p. cm. — (North to Alaska)
Includes index.
ISBN 1-55916-029-2
1. Alaska — Juvenile literature. [1. Alaska.] I. Title. II. Series:
Stone, Lynn M. North to Alaska.
F904.3.S765 1994
979.8'004—dc20 93-43981
CIP
AC

Printed in the USA

TABLE OF CONTENTS

PEOPLE OF ALASKA

Alaska's nearly 600,000 people come from many backgrounds and cultures. Alaskans may be black, white, Asian, Hispanic or Native American.

Most Alaskans in larger cities, like Anchorage, Fairbanks and Juneau, are white. Most people in the **remote** villages are Native Americans — Eskimos and American Indians.

Native Americans were the only Alaskans until the late 1700s. Then the first white settlers, from nearby Russia, came to Alaska.

Native Alaskans were the only Alaskans before the arrival of Russian traders in the 1700s

THE FIRST ALASKANS

The first Alaskans probably arrived about 20,000 years ago. They probably came to Alaska from Asia over an ancient "bridge" of land. Now covered by the Bering Sea, the "bridge" once linked Alaska with Russian Siberia.

Some of the earliest Alaskans were Inupiat and Yupik Eskimos, Aleuts, Athabaskans, Tlingits, Chugach, Haida and Koniags. Over time, these groups of Native Americans moved into many parts of Alaska.

A collection of crafts from Alaska's Native American groups

ALEUTS

The Aleuts are native people of the Alaska Peninsula and Aleutian Islands. They live in a stormy world of fog, rain, wind and tossing seas.

Like other Native Americans of Alaska, modern Aleuts live with a mixture of old and new ways. Native Americans fear that they will lose old customs, beliefs and crafts. The modern world is all around them, and they are becoming more and more a part of it.

The Aleuts settled in the stormy world of the Aleutian Islands

ESKIMOS

Eskimo people live mostly along the northern and western sea coasts of Alaska. Their **ancestors** depended upon wild animals for food and clothing. They hunted whales, seals, polar bears and **caribou.**

Today, airplanes bring many different foods and other things to Eskimo villages. Many Eskimos hunt from snowmobiles. Some still dare to hunt whales from skin-covered *umiak* boats, just as their ancestors did.

An Eskimo fishes through a hole in Arctic ice

Alaska gold miners of long ago at the snowy Chilkoot Pass

A totem pole in Southeast Alaska

OTHER NATIVE AMERICANS

The Tlingit and Haida groups of Native Americans settled in Southeast Alaska. They lived in wooden homes and became skillful carvers of wooden masks and **totem poles.** The 15,000 Tlingits are today the largest of Alaska's Native American groups.

The Athabaskans settled in the forests within Alaska. They hunted caribou, which supplied leather as well as meat.

An Athabaskan woman working at a fish camp along the Yukon River

THE RUSSIANS

The first white settlers in Alaska came from Russia. Many Russians were traders who hunted sea otters for their rich fur. By 1784, the Russians had a village on Kodiak Island.

The number of Russian villages grew. Russia soon claimed Alaska, which it called "Russian America."

Russia sold Alaska to the United States in 1867 for only $7,200,000. By then the sea otters were nearly gone, and Russia had problems at home.

Signs of the Russian years still live in some Alaskan churches, place names and in communities of Russian Alaskans.

Russian culture can be seen in the design of an Alaskan church

ACHEMAK AIR SERVICE
HOMER, AL

BUSH PILOTS

Alaskan bush pilots are an important and special group of people. Bush pilots fly small airplanes into Alaska's roadless wild back country — the "bush." Bush planes can land on water, snow or rough ground.

Bush planes carry hunters, fishermen, scientists, explorers, villagers and supplies. Sometimes bush pilots make daring rescues of people who are hurt or ill.

A bush pilot guns the throttle of his "Beaver" float plane

MUSHERS

Mushers are another special group of Alaskans. Mushers "drive" trained teams of dogs that pull sleds across the snow. Long ago, Alaskan natives began to use dog sleds for travel.

Mushers played an important part in Alaskan history in 1925. Their dog sleds brought diptheria medicine several hundred miles from Nenana north to Nome. The medicine saved many lives.

Today dog sleds are used mostly for fun and sport.

Musher (rear) drives his dog team and two passengers through the snow of Denali National Park

PROSPECTORS

Gold **prospectors,** or gold hunters, still pan for gold from Alaska creeks. However, there are few prospectors today. In the late 1890s, Alaska had thousands of prospectors. Gold had been found in Alaska and the Yukon Territory in Canada next door. Dreaming of instant riches, people rushed north.

By 1910, most of the gold — and dreams — were gone. Most of the gold seekers drifted back to the lower 48 states.

Glossary

ancestors (AN ses terz) — a person's grandparents, great-grandparents, and all other relatives who lived in the past

caribou (KARE uh boo) — large, northern cousins of deer, found in large herds; wild reindeer

prospector (PRAH spehk ter) — a person who hunts for gold or another mineral

remote (re MOTE) — somewhere far away or out-of-the-way

totem pole (TO tem POLE) — a wooden pole carved by Native Americans of the Northwest coast to remember certain people and events

INDEX